THE TORTOISE
AND
THE HORNED TOAD

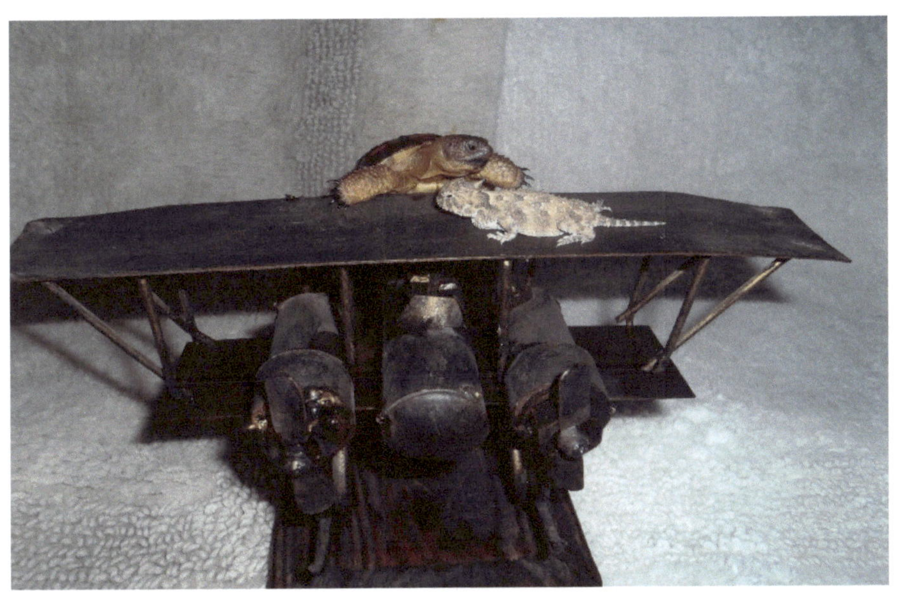

CLEOPATRA AND JULIO CESAR

CLEMENCIA SÁNCHEZ

Ghost Town Publishers House
P. O. Box 7
Johannesburg, Ca 93528

ghosttown395@gmail.com

ISBN-13: 978-1729739730
ISBN-10:1729739733

For the children of my children
and all the children of the world

Hi! As you can see, I'm a Tortoise. And here I'm roaming around as usual. Always curious and smelling everything as if I am a puppy.
My name is Cleopatra, a pleasure to meet you.

A long, long time ago, a girl named Yalitza and I got acquainted. She found me in the back yard of her house. I was lying on my back with my head and legs out of my shell, struggling to turn myself over. I was extremely desperately crying for help.

Not far from me a cat was staring at, as ready to attack me. When Yalitza saw the horrific scene, she ran to scare the cat away and she picked me up. I was very scared! When she picked me up, I, quickly, pulled my head and tiny limbs into my shell to hid myself.

Yalitza caressed and talked to me as if I were a baby. She held me warmly against her chest to comfort me and warm my tinny body. I was awfully cold! I was probably terrified after having so much trouble trying to turn myself right-side up, to escape from the cat.

Knowing that tortoise is vegetarian, Yalitza fed me some lettuce. I was very hungry! And rather than living me outside where the cat or any other predator would be looking for me, she kept me in her house where I would be safe and remain alive.

A year later, I met a horned toad.

He was also found in Yalitza's property. She was watering her garden when suddenly she saw a tiny lizard leaping from beneath of a plant, where it must have felt the water approaching it. It ran about two feet away from the water and suddenly it stopped. Then it ran back towards Yalitza's feet and stopped right on top of her toe.

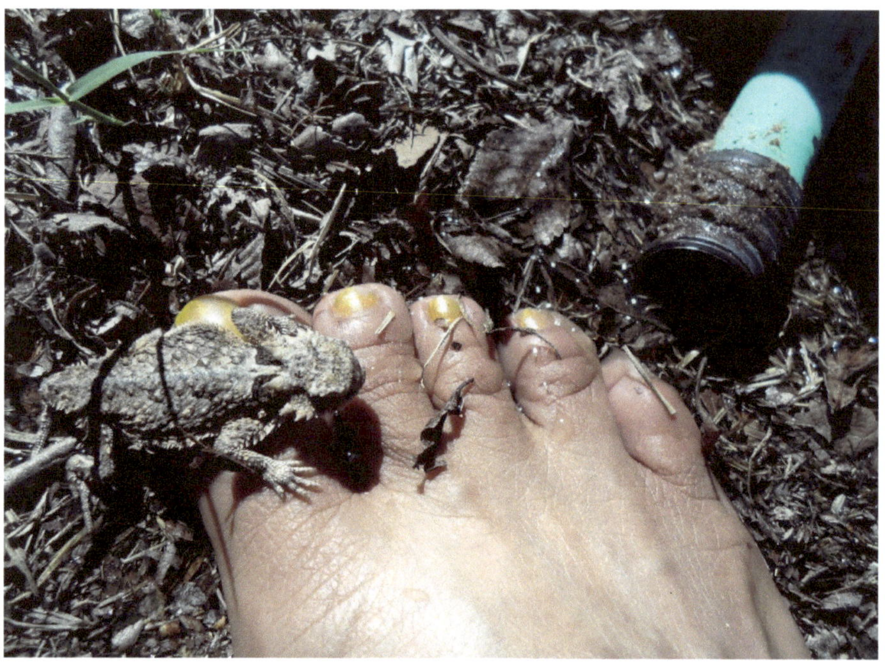

Here's horned toad. He's always ready for anything. He thinks he's as sharp as a smart kid in grammar school. He also says he's as fast as any lizard who would want to race him. But he prefers to run on his little yard than to be running around in dangerous terrain where a hungry coyote, a raven, a cat or a vicious dog, would devour him.

His name is Julio Cesar.

To see him so small and harmless, Yalitza picked him up and carried him in her hand. Thinking she would keep it only long enough until the water in the puddle would soak into the ground, so that the little creature wouldn't drown.

After having him in her hand for an hour, she decided to placed him by my side. We seemed to enjoy meeting each other. Don't you think?

After we met, I told him "I love being outdoors running, and feeling and eating grass, green grass." Julio Cesar looked at me as if I was crazy because he could see I'm so slow compared to him. I think we enjoyed meeting each other from the very moment we met because we got along like old pals.

At the beginning, Julio Cesar didn't call me by my name.
I think he couldn't pronounce my name. So instead of
calling me Cleopatra, he just calls me Cleo, because
when he wants to talk to me, he always says "Hey Cleo!"

Even though he is fast and I am slow, we got along alright, but Julio Cesar didn't seem to want to play with me, especially when I wanted to play marbles. Sometimes he even seemed a bit afraid of me, but that may have been because we weren't well acquainted yet, or perhaps because Julio is a carnivorous and I am a vegetarian, but he didn't know that.

But I didn't care who was at home with me, as long as I had someone to play with.
I got used to play with Canelo, Yalitza's dog. Possibly because I always had him under control.

Julio Cesar was wild and demanding. Just by the looks of his eyes, I can tell when he's asking for food. And if he doesn't get it soon enough, he gets antsy like any spoiled kid.
"I want some food, I'm hungry, either I get some or I'll climb up this wall and get it myself!"

I do understand that Julio Cesar needs time to get adjusted to his new home and his new family member that's why I tried to gave him a littler space in my hose. Here we are. This is my casita. I cleaned up my mess and put up some flowers because he's paying me a visit, but he has his own pad where he prefers to sleep alone.

Finally, a few weeks after we met, Julio Cesar and I had become real good friends. One day he got very close to me because he wanted to tell me something.

"Hey Cleo, I truly like you. You're my kind of tortoise, but if I were a punk rocker, I'd tell you you're a cool, dude. I really think you're awesome! But I'm no punk rocker. I can't even play a musical instrument, but a few times when I've been very scared, I've been able to whistle."

Now Julio Cesar feels safe in his surroundings. He gets lots of love from Yelitza. She takes good care of me and him, and being both cold blooded reptiles, we love the warm human hands. Julio Cesar and I loves to be outdoors. I eat whatever green I can find. Julio Cesar only eats ants, but we both enjoy getting sunshine as most kids enjoy at the beach.

During Summer, most of the time, Julio Cesar and I are out playing in the back yard and having fun together. He gets exited and jumps around happily shrilling like many little boys and girls.
"Cleopatra, look at me, I'm riding the bird! Can you see me? You want to ride it? I can get off and you can ride it, but you're much heavier than me. I hope you don't squish it."

Yalitza's always hunting ants for Julio Cesar. That makes him very happy because he knows he'll get plenty to eat. He loves to eat ants, especially the larger red ones. He's not too keen on the black ones, could be because they don't have enough meat and juice. Every time he's going to eat his lunch, he become joyful.
"It's time for my lunch," Julio hollered, "I am going to wash my hands because they're dirty and I don't want to get sick. I'm awfully hungry! Mmm huh, the lunch looks delicious; it looks so finger licking good."

I'm not like him, I always have all kinds of vegetables in my tray. I love them. I especially like spinach, which I had never tasted before I met Yalitza. Ever since I began to enjoy spinach, my muscles have been growing just like those of Popeye the sailor man. I love fresh vegetables. They make me healthy, smart, and strong like the Wander Woman. I eat them every day, especially when they're in season. That's when they taste the best, and they're nice and juicy and crispy too.

I also enjoy taking a shower every day like many kids do so I can be clean all the time, but I cannot bathe daily. I can bathe only once every other week because I am a tortoise and I don't want to get sick. But when Yalitza showers me, the water makes me feel clean, fresh, shiny, happy and relaxed, um huh, I love it.

Julio Cesar is not afraid of me anymore. He even allows me to kiss him in its cheek. Of course, he was a bit shy the first time I tried to kiss him because he'd never been kissed before, but eventually he gave in, and now he kisses me regularly. One day I told him, Julio Cesar, I love you and I love to play with you. Let me hug you.
"Now wait a minute, Cleo! First, I let you kiss me in my cheek, now you want to hug me, too," he uttered.

About a month later, one day in November, after most of the leaves had fallen from trees, I didn't wake up from my sleep. Yalitza became worried about it. Even though I wasn't awake the next day, Yalitza took me outside and placed me on the ground. She wanted me to get some sunshine so I would wake up to play with Julio. But I had no desire to play. I just wanted to sleep and dream about pretty flowers all around me.

When I opened my eyes, I saw Julio Cesar looking at me as if he felt there was something wrong with me. Then he run and jumped all over me till he put his head under me tummy. I knew he wanted to play with me, but I was too sleepy to play.
"Cleo, Cleo, Cleo I'm glad you came out! I was worried about you. I haven't seen you for three days. Would you like to play with me? I wanna play with you, Cleo, common wake up!"

When I didn't respond, Julio Cesar got close to my ear and whispered.
"Cleo, will you wake up? I wanna play with you. If you want to, you can choose the game you want to play. We can even play hide-and- go-seek, kick the can or tag." I didn't wake up.

Then Julio Cesar started pushing me from my side pleading me.

"Cleo, wake up, please. What's wrong with you? You sick or somethin'? Maybe I should call a tortoise doctor."

He pushed me from behind. He pushed and pushed, but I didn't wake up. Julio Cesar fells disappointed.
"Wake up, Cleo! Andale andale, muchacha (hurry hurry, girl) I wanna play with you, muevete (move it)" He started saying something in Spanish. I was glad I was able to understand him, but he didn't know it.

I didn't move a bit. Then, Julio Cesar went back to my other side and pushed me again without success.
"Cleo don't be cruel to me; you have to help me move you. I'm not strong enough to move you alone! I'm just a little guy who wants to play with an old pall and you're a big husky tortoise who don't want to wake up!"

Then I started moving away from Julio Cesar because he was disturbing my sleep. Julio Cesar thought I didn't know what I was doing.
"Cleo, don't move that way, go to the other way! There is lots of water and you don't know how to swim. Still you sleep?"

Finally, Julio Cesar became annoyed, so he stepped in front of me.

"You are very lazy, Cleo. You just want to sleep. I don't understand why you don't want play with me today? You don't want me to be your friend anymore?"

Then, I open my eyes and holded Julio Cesar's right arm
with my left arm.
"Listen Julio Cesar, I still love you and yes, I always want
to play with you, but you have to let me sleep! Its
November, it's time for me to hibernate! Don't you
know I have to sleep?" Then, he walked out pensive and
I slept another day, all day long.

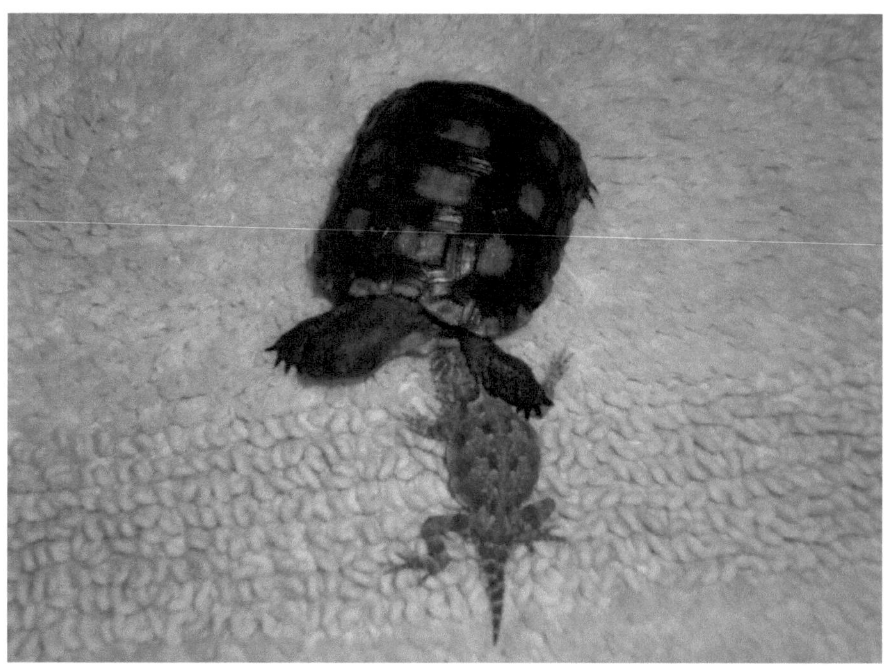

The next day, even though I was sleeping, I felt hungry. When I woke up to eat something, I noticed Julio Cesar was there, waiting for me to wake up to play. As soon I opened one eye, he put his tiny arm on my head and laydown on his tiny stomach so he would apologize. "I'm sorry, Cleo. Now, I capich. (understand) Will you forgive me? I wasn't aware that you hibernate just like bears. I didn't know it was November already. Sometimes I lose track of time. I don't have a calendar and I don't have an iPhone either."

After I accepted his apologize, he kissed me on my cheek like old pals from the desert.
"Don't worry, Julio Cesar. If nobody had never explained to you about tortoise's life, It's not your fault. Come on, I will give you a ride before I completely hibernate. You have been a good friend to me. So, hop on little buddy!

Then Julio Cesar, excited, jumped on my back. And I
started giving him a ride around our little park. He was
the happiest lizard I have ever met in all my entire life.
He felt as if he was a tuff cowboy.
"Yupiiiii, this is fun, Cleo! ¡Hi yo, Silver! Away, Cleo!
Thank you so much. You're awesome! I'm sorry you
have to sleep all winter, but I have to respect your
culture. See you next year! I'll be here waiting for you to
play again. I love you, Cleo, and don't you forget it
you're my best buddyyyy!!!!"

THE END